Faded Glory

The Bradford, Queensbury, Halifax, Thornton & Keighley lines

Willowherb Publishing

First published 2020

Willowherb Publishing
www.willowherbpublishing.co.uk

© **Alan Whitaker and Jan Rapacz 2020**

The authors would welcome any colour and/or black and white images relating to railways in the Bradford, Halifax and Keighley areas for possible publication in future titles. Please send details to Willowherb Publishing, PO Box 160, Manchester, M9 9AN or email: willowherbpublishing@hotmail.com if you are able to offer suitable material or require more information.

Printed in the UK by:
The Amadeus Press
Cleckheaton
BD19 4TQ
ISBN: 978-0-9935678-6-5

Front Cover
With rosebay willowherb in profusion, B1 Class 4-6-0 No. 61016 *Inyala* crosses Queensbury Viaduct with a light load from Thornton to Laisterdyke on a glorious summer afternoon in 1964. (*Howard Malham*)

Frontispiece
The construction of the majestic 17-arch viaduct at Hewenden, between Wilsden and Cullingworth, was recorded in an illuminated album presented to the contractor, Isaac Woodiwiss, on completion of the railway from Bradford to Keighley in 1884. (*Jan Rapacz Collection*)

Rear Cover
Track-lifting had reached Hewenden Viaduct in August 1964, with the Down line already partly recovered. Track panels are being lifted by a crane and placed on bogie bolster wagons standing on the Up line. (*D. J. Mitchell*)

Introduction

This is a book of recognition and remembrance – not just for the lost railway network it features, but also for those who battled through hostile terrain to build it and for those who then faced the often difficult challenges of operating it.

In particular, it is dedicated to the railway men and women of the 1950s and 60s who worked tirelessly to serve their customers while struggling day after day with outdated equipment in decrepit workplaces while their bosses undermined them by turning away business at stations, depots and from entire lines that they wanted to close.

This tried and tested strategy usually involved reducing demand by withdrawing services and operational support and starving lines of all but the most essential maintenance so spending on an increasing backlog of infrastructure renewals could not be economically justified. The interests of customers were just an aside.

The fact that the national railway network was haemorrhaging cash is not in dispute. Nor is the fact that trying to stem the losses was essential - but the tactics adopted by the railway hierarchy to achieve their aims at a time when scrutiny was far less intense than it is today did them no favours and resulted in a loss of public trust which lasted for years.

However, it was an approach that suited their agenda as they were under political pressure to cut the deficit which they themselves had increased with some very ill-judged policy decisions conjured up to grab the attention of duplicitous MPs who were more interested in road building than railways.

The period covered by this book was not one of the most distinguished in British railway history, as will be seen by the photographic evidence between these covers. The sight of rundown stations and goods depots did not present British Railways in a professional light - or instill confidence - and it showed in the balance sheet as more and more business was driven away.

In purely economic terms, the withdrawal of passenger services from the former Great Northern lines linking Bradford and Halifax with Keighley via Queensbury was very probably justified as loadings were light. However, the closure in May 1955 was enacted hastily without any effort to reduce costs by trying out the new cheaper-to-run, faster and more attractive Diesel Multiple Units which were just entering service.

Instead, senior managers claimed the new trains would not be able to tackle the steep gradients – a bizarre and ridiculous excuse as some of the newly-delivered DMUs were already operating on steeply graded lines elsewhere and they went on to have a long career working on such routes. Indeed, the Queensbury line was used to train drivers on the new DMUs, both before and after it closed to passengers - and they performed admirably.

Whether the use of the new diesel units would have saved the passenger services in the longer term is debatable, though. They were tried on the neighbouring Keighley & Worth Valley line a few years later to see whether they could boost passenger numbers but the modest increase in patronage was not deemed to be sufficient and the service was withdrawn at the end of 1961.

But freight was a completely different matter. Movement of goods was the principal reason the Great Northern Railway drove its lines through the uplands to Halifax and Keighley in the first place and, although railway freight revenues had begun to decline after the war, there was still a healthy local demand.

That did not impress BR management. Having got rid of the passenger services, they then withdrew 'through' freight a year later and severed the route by closing two short sections. What they had not bargained for was an upsurge in new freight business - secured after closure to passenger trains - which brought a brief 'golden age' to some of the depots that continued to operate.

One particularly profitable new traffic flow was the movement of pre-cast concrete beams from a plant at Cullingworth which began in 1959. These were used in motorway bridge building and led to sidings being reopened and additional staff being recruited. But it did not suit BR's agenda and, early in 1963, the regional commercial department pulled the plug on the traffic by claiming that there were insufficient bogie bolster wagons available to carry the long beams. That left the way clear to close Cullingworth goods yard nine months later - along with neighbouring Wilsden - and cut the line back to Thornton.

Miraculously, there was a sudden surfeit of bogie bolster wagons the following year when they were needed to carry redundant track panels lifted from the closed section.

The spectacular nature of the 'Queensbury Lines' network was also its Achilles heel. With tunnels, viaducts, deep cuttings, high embankments and bridges abounding, the maintenance liabilities were significant. Track relaying, tunnel repairs and a few bridge renewals were carried out in the 1930s, after which nothing but essential maintenance was done and that, in the final reckoning, killed it.

It was sound economics, driven by local industrialists, which led to the building of the network in the 1870s and 1880s and it was dubious economics that led to its premature demise. That could also be said of other lines which fell by the wayside as a result of the same practices.

Many of these lines would undoubtedly have closed in any case as the country's economy and transport needs changed in the 1970s and 80s but some, including the Queensbury Lines, were run down with undue haste at a time when the freight business was clearly healthy and there was potential for more.

This is the third in the *Great Northern Outpost* series of full colour albums from Willowherb Publishing covering the *Bradford & Thornton* and the *Halifax, Thornton and Keighley Railways* and their associated branches. The vast majority of the photographs in this new collection have never been previously published and many have only recently come to light.

As the son of the last Thornton Station Master, I grew up alongside the line and was in a unique position to witness the highs and lows in the years leading to closure. I have again delved into my own personal records - and those of my late father from his time at Thornton between 1951 and 1964 - to support the captions with information not made public before. For his part, my co-author Jan Rapacz, who grew up next to the line at Great Horton, has trawled his extensive files to provide the historical foundation for the book.

Once again, we are indebted to the few photographers who recorded the dying days of the 'Queensbury Lines' in colour at a time when most took their cameras to more exciting main line locations.

Halifax and Keighley were true Great Northern outposts linked to Bradford by some of the most spectacularly engineered railway infrastructure in the country and, although this book only shows its decline, there are still defiant hints of its former glory. Its faded glory.

Alan Whitaker

June 2020

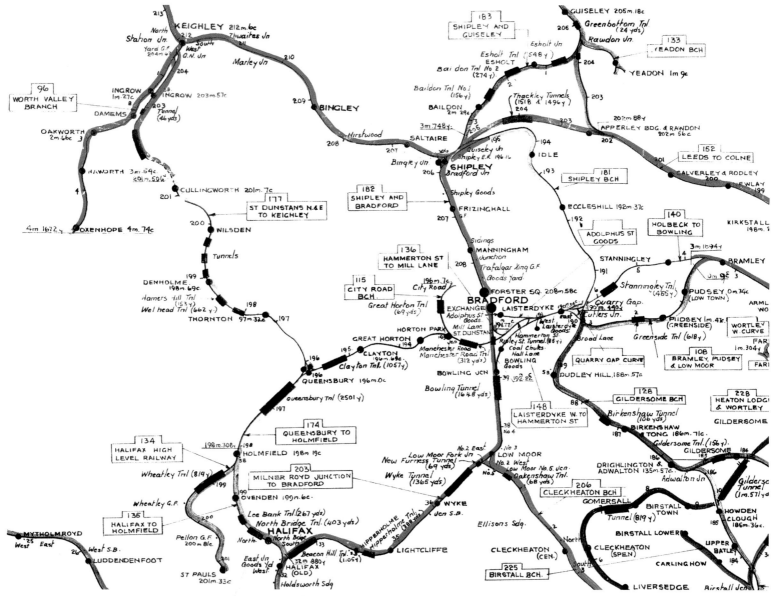

This British Railways West Riding Permanent Way Inspectors' diagram dates from 1956 and is colour-coded to highlight areas of responsibility. The section from St. Dunstan's to a mile beyond Cullingworth was covered by the Laisterdyke inspector, with the rest of the line to Keighley under the supervision of his counterpart based at Shipley. The Halifax to Holmfield and High Level lines were the responsibility of the Sowerby Bridge P-Way inspector. *(Jan Rapacz Collection)*

The austere façade of Bradford Exchange station soaks up the late summer sun as the last ever passenger train to Queensbury and Thornton prepares to depart from Platform 6 at 1025 a.m. on Sunday, 6 September 1964. The train, chartered by the West Riding Branch of the Railway Correspondence and Travel Society (RCTS), comprised a two-car Metropolitan Cammell Diesel Multiple Unit coupled to a three-car Birmingham Railway and Carriage Works 'Calder Valley' set. It was to be the first passenger train to traverse the Queensbury line since closure to passenger services nine years earlier and it would leave its mark in history as the last. The 10-platform Exchange station was constructed by the Lancashire & Yorkshire Railway to replace an earlier facility which was too cramped for the number of trains timetabled to use it. Five platforms were reserved for the Great Northern Railway Company's trains and their portion of the new station opened on 27 September 1886. The five L&YR platforms which made up the other half were all in use by August 1888. Water columns stand guard on the platforms, ready to replenish the numerous steam locomotives still hauling passenger services to and from Bradford at that time. (*Arthur Wilson*)

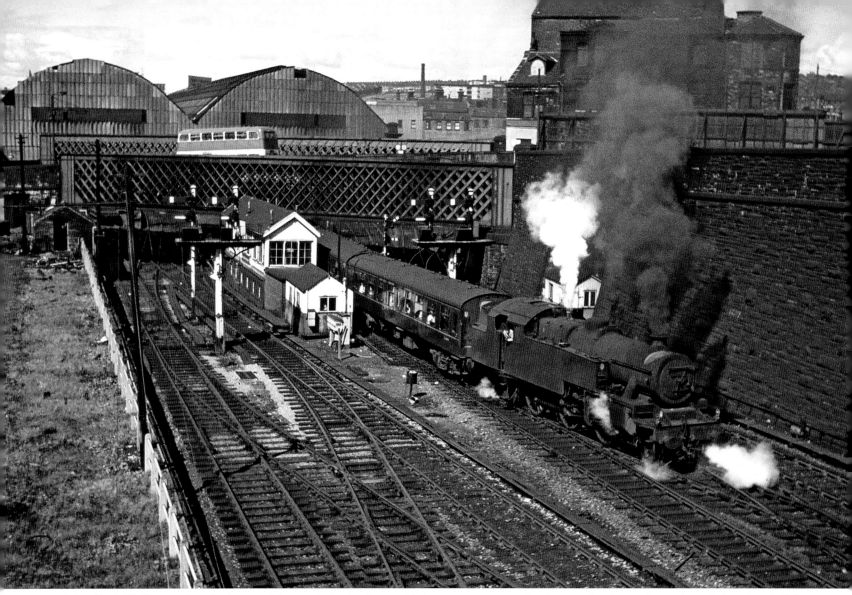

A Bradford City Transport motor bus provides a splash of colour amid the drab greyness of the railway infrastructure as it heads down Bridge Street, while Wakefield-based Stanier 2-6-4T No. 42650 sets about the climb from Exchange station with the Bradford portion of the 3.05 p.m. service to London King's Cross on 8 August 1966. To compound its neglected appearance, the locomotive has a burned smokebox top but it was obviously in better shape than it looked as it continued in service for another ten months. Bradford Interchange, which opened in January 1973 to replace Exchange station, now occupies the area in front of the bridge. (*Peter Fitton*)

A rather fine GNR lattice signal was a surprising survivor at St Dunstan's at the time of this view in July 1966. It marked the junction of the lines to Laisterdyke and Leeds with those to Queensbury, Halifax and Keighley. Photographer John Rothera has captured this evocative scene from a London-bound train as it takes the line towards Leeds, passing in front of the last remaining signal box at the site of St. Dunstan's station which had closed in 1952. A part of the original platform ramp can be glimpsed in front of the signal box and the former Station Master's house can be seen just above - and to the left of - the signal box roof. (*John Rothera*)

St Dunstan's station was constructed in a triangular layout with separate signal boxes controlling each of the three junctions. However, platforms were only provided on the Bradford to Laisterdyke and Bradford to Thornton sections. The station opened on 21 November 1878 but its importance as an interchange point for Leeds and Wakefield main line services and those coming in from the Queensbury direction gradually diminished and it closed on 15 September 1952. Most of the buildings were removed soon afterwards, leaving the last surviving signal box, seen here, and a couple of wooden cabins as reminders of better days. The box was still operational at the time of this view in July 1972 but closed five months later, on 4 December. Until 1924, it had controlled the North Junction only but then became responsible for the whole of the St. Dunstan's triangle when the East and West Junction boxes were closed as part of a signalling rationalisation scheme. The disused and overgrown lines diverging to the right of the signal box once took passengers to and from Queensbury, Thornton and beyond. *(Clive Weston)*

Bradford Exchange station did not have any engine release crossovers at the buffer stops so empty trains often had to be reversed back up the line to St. Dunstan's where the triangle was used to turn the whole ensemble. The stock was then propelled back downgrade and into its allotted platform to form its next service. A maximum of five coaches was permitted to be propelled from St Dunstan's North Junction to St Dunstan's West Junction in good visibility. A Stanier 'Black Five' is seen here doing just that on Saturday 28 May 1966, with the photographer standing on the remains of the Queensbury platform. Until closure of the station, passengers from the Queensbury line would change here for trains to Laisterdyke and beyond. After that, they had no option but to continue into Bradford Exchange to pick up their connections but this was only short lived as passenger services from Keighley and Halifax via Queensbury were withdrawn in 1955. After 12 years of disuse, the Queensbury line platforms at St. Dunstan's were finally removed in July 1967. (D.J. Mitchell)

On the same day as the previous view, a Birmingham Railway and Carriage Works (BRCW) Diesel Multiple Unit drops down the gradient from Hammerton Street and passes St. Dunstan's East Junction on a service from Leeds to Liverpool via Bradford Exchange. With their distinctive raised outer cab windows, these iconic trains - first introduced in 1961 - were known locally as 'Calder Valley' units. They were classified as Class 110 under British Rail's TOPS scheme in the late 1960s and remained a familiar sight on Trans-Pennine services between York and Manchester via Leeds and Bradford until their displacement by new generation units in the late 1980s. For a number of years, all the Class 110s were allocated to Bradford's Hammerton Street diesel depot until its closure in May 1984. They were then transferred to Leeds Neville Hill depot where they saw out the rest of their working lives. The short connection from the original Leeds, Bradford and Halifax Junction line to the L&YR at Mill Lane required extensive excavations to create a deep cutting with high retaining walls, part of which can be seen behind the DMU. This view was taken from the top of St. Dunstan's Tunnel on the Bradford and Thornton Railway. *(D.J. Mitchell)*

A Fairburn tank locomotive working bunker-first on the Bradford to Leeds portion of another service to London King's Cross passes St. Dunstan's East Junction where the Bradford and Thornton line diverges through the tunnel under Ripley Terrace. At the time of this view in April 1967, the line was only open for goods as far as Horton Park and City Road. Unusually, the former signal cabin controlling this junction was situated on top of the tunnel so the signalmen could see up the line towards Laisterdyke. The signalling here was rationalised and concentrated on the remaining North Junction signal box from 1924. *(D.J. Mitchell)*

This is the other side of St. Dunstan's Tunnel on the connecting spur from the Bradford and Leeds line. This section never had any platforms despite a short-lived direct service from Laisterdyke to Thornton being introduced on the opening of the Bradford and Thornton Railway for passengers in October 1878. A tunnel was needed at this location to facilitate the junction of Ripley Terrace and Eldon Street on the edge of the Ripleyville model village, built to house employees of a large nearby dyeworks. (D.J. Mitchell)

Having left its coaches in the former GNR carriage sidings, an unidentified Ivatt Mogul 2-6-0 locomotive emerges from the bridge under the L&YR main line to Halifax as it runs around its train. It would then propel the stock back down the gradient into Bradford Exchange station. A few covered wagons, parcels vans and brake vans can be seen in the former L&YR carriage sidings beyond the stabled coaching stock. These sidings were accessed from the L&Y main line and were controlled from Mill Lane signal box. The short 'engine siding' on the left was laid to hold locomotives used for assisting heavy freight trains on the climb towards Horton Junction and Queensbury but this requirement had all but disappeared by the late 1940s. (D.J. Mitchell)

Looking back to St Dunstan's from Ripley Street, a freight working from City Road and Horton Park heads towards Laisterdyke on 20 July 1972. The train is hauled by one of Hammerton Street depot's Class 08 diesel shunters and comprises a crane, a couple of open wagons with recovered permanent way materials, empty mineral wagons and the obligatory brake van bringing up the rear. The GNR carriage sidings to the left became redundant when steam locomotive operation ended in Bradford at the end of September 1967, thereby removing the need for engines to run around empty coaching stock. On the weekend of 29 and 30 April 1972, the west to north lines, the carriage sidings and the banker siding at St. Dunstan's were all spiked out of use. The last goods traffic to and from Horton Park and City Road ran in August 1972 and St. Dunstan's signal box was taken out of use four months later. The Lady Well Mill of J.W. Firth Ltd., commission wool combers, is prominent in the background on the right. The mill was still in production at the time of writing, having survived the decimation of Bradford's woollen and worsted industry which once led the world. (Clive Weston)

An interesting view from under the L&YR main line, looking back towards St. Dunstan's West Junction in August 1965. This was actually the lowest point on the Bradford and Thornton Railway and was prone to flooding. The building next to the Down line is the truncated remains of the West Junction signal box which closed in 1924 when control of all movements around the St. Dunstan's triangle switched to the North Junction box. The redundant West box was then reduced in height and continued to fulfil a useful role as a platelayers' cabin until the demise of the line to Horton Park and City Road almost 50 years later. *(John Rothera)*

Having secured the previous view, photographer John Rothera turned his camera towards the 85 yards long Ripley Street Tunnel, seen here curving to the right towards Manchester Road. Due to the curvature of the line and difficulties in seeing signals for the junction ahead, the crews of trains approaching St Dunstan's from the Manchester Road direction were provided with a couple of low level colour light signals at this location. These can be seen on the right in front of the two equipment cabinets. A standard disc signal stands guard on the other line for the crossover and access to the carriage sidings. (*John Rothera*)

Closure of the lines from Keighley and Halifax to Bradford via Queensbury was implemented in stages, starting in 1956 when 'through' freight traffic was diverted away. As all passenger services had been withdrawn the previous year, this left the way clear for British Railways to dispense with the sections between Holmfield and Queensbury and Ingrow East and Cullingworth. Further closures in 1960, 1963 and 1965 left the coal sidings at Horton Park, the goods depot at Bradford City Road and a short section between Halifax and North Bridge as the only remaining parts of the 'Queensbury Lines' network still operational into the 1970s. Here, Class 08 diesel shunter No. 3294 heads a return working from City Road and Horton Park to Laisterdyke through the site of Manchester Road station which had closed in 1915. The date is 29 June 1972 and the load is typical of the time, comprising a Ferryvan and empty mineral wagons. Two months later, this traffic would be withdrawn and the line closed. The steel beams supported on concrete pipes formed a trough to carry utilities over the railway in advance of the widening of Manchester Road which began in February 1972 and took more than three years to complete. A portion of the original station building, still standing almost 60 years after closure, is just visible on the extreme left but it was on borrowed time. (Stuart Baker)

An unidentified B1 4-6-0 locomotive runs tender first towards Manchester Road Tunnel with a rake of mineral wagons loaded with scrap from City Road in 1966. This long established traffic, destined for South Yorkshire, originated at this time from scrap merchants George Cohen Sons & Company Ltd. who had taken over from a previous operator in 1965. The movement of scrap from City Road yard provided a steady revenue stream for British Railways and it continued almost until the closure of the line in 1972. The tall chimney is part of St Luke's Hospital, which was erected in 1852 as the Bradford Union Workhouse and Infirmary to the designs of local architects Henry Lockwood and William Mawson, who also designed Bradford Town Hall. Originally known as the City of Bradford Municipal General Hospital, the name St Luke's started to be used from the late 1920s and was officially adopted when it became part of the National Health Service in 1948. On the left is the All Saints Church of England Primary School. (Bert Perry)

A view from under the Laisteridge Lane overbridge looking down the 1 in 50 gradient towards Manchester Road Tunnel, with the Horton Junction Up advance home signal on the left. This viewpoint, close to the rail level, shows that the 312 yards long tunnel was not particularly deep underground. It was filled with a concrete plug in the late 1980s to provide secure foundations for a new hospital extension which was built on top of it. A treadle bar can be seen in the 'four foot' of the Down line. This worked in conjunction with the rodding for the facing point lock at the junction and prevented the lock being released and the points changed when a train wheel depressed the bar. (*John Rothera*)

Still under the Laisteridge Lane bridge - but looking the other way - we see Horton Junction and the main line to Great Horton rising towards the abandoned platforms and footbridge of Horton Park station, closed in 1952. The signal box on the left controlled the junction of the goods branch to City Road and access to the coal yard sidings at Horton Park. The difference in gradients is very obvious as the main line continues to ascend at 1 in 50 while the City Road branch diverges off to the right on a 1 in 86 falling gradient. This view dates from July 1965, a few weeks after the line to Great Horton and Thornton had closed. (*John Rothera*)

Horton Junction signal box was constructed to a rather low and squat design to ensure that signalling staff had an unimpeded view under Laisteridge Lane bridge and down to Manchester Road Tunnel. It was commissioned in August 1877 to replace a temporary ground frame installed after opening of the City Road goods branch eight months earlier. Because of its junction status and the frequency of traffic on the branch, it became the last operational signal box on the entire 'Queensbury Lines' network. In August 1961, it still required double shifts on weekdays and one on Saturdays. The weekday shifts began at 6 a.m. and the box remained open until after the passing of the last freight train from City Road at 6.49 p.m. On Saturdays, a single shift operated between 6 a.m. and 1.20 p.m. It was closed on Sundays as there was no traffic. Horton Junction signal box was originally fitted with a 24-lever frame which was replaced in 1901 by a 30-lever Saxby & Farmer frame, to which an additional lever was added some time later. It was reduced to a ground frame in February 1967, with the junction set for City Road as the line to Great Horton had been closed and lifted by that time. This view dates from 30 June 1966 when the box was still fully operational. *(Geoff Brown)*

The interior of Horton Junction signal box in July 1965, showing the lever frame to good effect. The spur line from the Horton Park coal yard sidings was provided with a set of buffer stops instead of a Catch Point at its junction with the Up main line and these can just be seen through the signal box windows. The red and yellow levers controlled the Stop and Distant signals, while the black levers activated the points. The blue lever controlled a facing point lock, the white levers with black chevrons were for placing emergency detonators on the running lines and the plain white levers were spares. The two levers set for traffic in the 'pulled' position are numbers 17 and 18 which controlled the junctions for the City Road branch. Lever number 19 was the facing point lock for point number 18. (*John Rothera*)

A superb panorama of City Road goods yard with its impressive bank of 24 double coal drops and the Great Northern Railway warehouse beyond. This photograph was taken on the occasion of the RCTS West Riding Rail Tour on Sunday, 6 September 1964 which brought a passenger train to City Road for the first time since 1891 when excursions used the yard in connection with the Yorkshire Agricultural Show, being held nearby. The City Road 'pilot' locomotive – on this occasion a Class 03 diesel shunter – can be seen awaiting resumption of its weekday duties. This 25-acre site had a total of six miles of sidings and it remained an important rail freight hub at a time when other local yards were in decline. The amount of shunting required on a daily basis meant that City Road retained its allocated 'pilot' until 1967, after which the locomotives operating the daily trip freights took on the task. The Bradford Beck, seen running in the open alongside the coal merchants' huts, was once the most polluted watercourse in the city but is now much cleaner and is culverted over at this location, which is now occupied by a mail order distribution warehouse. (*John M. Ryan*)

Passengers hurry back to the waiting West Riding 'Special' to continue their tour of various freight-only lines in the Bradford and Huddersfield areas. The train had earlier visited Queensbury and Thornton before heading down the City Road branch. This view, looking towards Thornton Road, shows the overhead gantry crane used for a scrap metal business that operated from City Road yard and generated regular train loads of scrap, one of which was seen on Page 18. A classic GNR yard gas lamp still clinging on to a faded coat of 'oriental blue' - the colour favoured by the British Railways North Eastern Region for its various buildings, gates and other sundry structures - stands defiantly as an air of terminal decline exudes all around it. (*J.C.W. Halliday*)

The mixed traffic B1 Class 4-6-0s were frequent visitors to City Road yard from 1963 until their demise in 1967. This example is 61306, seen with a solitary mineral wagon in July 1967 - not long after its transfer to Bradford's Low Moor shed from Hull. Low Moor was the last shed in the country to operate B1s and had two others on its books at the time but 61306 was by far the best of the trio in terms of condition. The locomotive is standing in front of the extensive wool combing and dye works founded by Isaac Holden, one of the original promotors of the Bradford and Thornton Railway. Like many other local industrialists, Holden recognised that rail access was essential to the continued growth of his business as the delivery of raw materials would be cheaper and quicker and the dispatch of finished goods would also cost much less. The vast Alston Works was established alongside Thornton Road in 1864 and, until 1951, had several private siding connections into City Road yard. *(Peter Fitton)*

B1 No. 61306 is seen on another of its regular visits to City Road, this time shunting and placing a mixture of standard BR mineral and hopper wagons over the coal drops. The number of coal merchants receiving their deliveries at City Road was always substantial. The maximum recorded was 20 in 1928 and even at the time of this view in July 1967, eight still remained customers of the railway. Among them was Metcalfe and Vickers who specialised in house coals – especially 'nutty slack' which was a cheap fuel consisting of slack (coal dust) and small lumps of coal (nuts). Smoke emission from this slack, burned in open domestic grates, was greater than any other type of coal and was a prime cause of smoke-fog (or smog) which often blanketed Bradford during the autumn and winter months. The last of the very severe city smogs descended one afternoon in early December 1962 reducing visibility in places to barely three yards. (*Alan Thompson*)

City Road goods depot had a long association with 204 horsepower diesel shunters of Classes 03 and 04 which were used to shunt the yard and haul local trips to and from Laisterdyke. Due to the weight of some of the movements, they were often doubled up to provide increased braking and pulling power, coupled cab to cab. From October 1964, the City Road 'pilot' was also used on the twice weekly coal trip to Thornton which ran on Tuesdays and Thursdays until June 1965 and was always a light load well within the capability of a single 204hp unit. Later, Hammerton Street began to receive an allocation of more powerful Class 08 locomotives and these were soon pressed into service on the City Road duties. This example is seen here on 6 April 1972 alongside two Continental wooden-bodied long wheelbase Ferryvans. These were used for Cross-Channel freight which was distributed from a local warehouse. The vans operated under the International Vehicle Regulation (RIV or Regolamento Internazionale dei Veicoli) which was defined in 1922 to regulate the standards required for rail wagons operating across European boundaries. (Clive Weston)

Although City Road Goods Depot was downgraded to an unstaffed Public Delivery Siding in June 1967, business remained brisk for a variety of both inward and outward traffic and this continued into the early 1970s. However, BR had no long term commitment to the depot and the infrastructure was left to deteriorate. Track condition became so poor that nine derailments requiring the Hammerton Street breakdown crew were recorded in the yard between May 1968 and February 1971 – five of which were on the coal drops siding alone. Both City Road and Horton Park depots had been due to close on 31 July 1972 but this was unexpectedly put back by a month and the last trains ran in the week ending 26 August. In this view, taken a few days before the original closure date and with several photographers in attendance, Class 08 D3547 is about to depart from City Road, having made up its train. The locomotive is still carrying the 'D' (diesel) prefix to its number which was becoming rare by this time. BR had issued a directive that the prefix should be painted out on all its diesel fleet after the end of steam in 1968 as it was no longer necessary. *(www.the-transport-photo-interchange.co.uk)*

Having arrived at Horton Junction with a train of scrap metal from City Road, B1 No. 61306 has been detached and prepares to collect empties from Horton Park coal yard in July 1967. It was customary for any wagons brought up from City Road to be left on the Up branch line between All Saints Road and the junction while the engine attended to its duties in the yard. Here, the driver is awaiting permission to enter the sidings which are being checked by the guard seen walking up the spur line in the distance. The main line tracks to Great Horton and beyond had been lifted a year before this photograph was taken, leaving just Horton Park yard and the City Road branch as the last remnants of the old Bradford and Thornton Railway. (*Peter Fitton*)

A few days after the view on the previous page, 61306 was back at Horton Park where it is seen in the yard preparing to collect empty wagons. Following closure of Great Horton in June 1965, some of the local coal merchants began to receive their supplies at Horton Park where new coal hoppers were installed to cope with the increased patronage. Some sidings were also lifted to provide extra stacking space, leaving only two of the original seven on this site still in operation. As this is the last time we will see 61306 in this book, it is worth mentioning that, after withdrawal from BR service in the early hours of 2 October 1967 – the last B1 to go - it went on to become one of only two of the 410-strong class to avoid scrapping. It now carries the name Mayflower which was originally bestowed on its less fortunate classmate No. 61379 which was cut up in 1962. *(John S. Whiteley)*

A powerful view of Class 08 No. D3547 as it propels five loaded mineral wagons up the spur line from Horton Junction and into the coal yard on Friday, 14 July 1972. This locomotive, which had spent 11 years in Scotland from new, was transferred to Hammerton Street depot in January 1971 after a short spell at Leeds Holbeck. It had the dubious distinction of being the last loco to derail in Horton Park yard before its closure in August 1972. As at City Road, referred to earlier, track condition in the yard had become very poor in its last few years of operation and derailments of wagons and locos were not uncommon. The signal box, by now only operated as a ground frame to permit movements in and out of the coal sidings, had lost its Horton Junction name boards and was beginning to look dilapidated, in keeping with the rest of the surrounding railway environment. Looking back, it all seems rather depressing but, at the time, there was a resigned acceptance as British Rail's management let things run down so closure of depots on their hit-list could be achieved without much fuss. *(Gerald Baxter)*

Having delivered the loaded wagons seen in the previous photograph, D3547 eases the day's empties from Horton Park to be attached to the empty hopper wagons from City Road which can be seen waiting on the left. These 20-ton capacity vehicles were particularly favoured for City Road coal traffic as they could be shunted over the coal drops to discharge their payloads from flaps underneath, whereas standard 16-ton mineral wagons with drop side doors were a better choice for locations not having any coal drops, such as Horton Park. *(Gerald Baxter)*

The laying of carriage sidings at Horton Park in 1897 necessitated the extension of the station footbridge to provide safe access to the platforms from the All Saints Road direction. After closure of the station to regular passenger trains in September 1952, this access was no longer needed as the only exit for any special workings for sports events was on the other side at Horton Park Avenue. The extension to the footbridge was, therefore, dismantled leaving the original section intact, as seen here in 1966. The intricate ironwork of the balustrades contrasts with the rugged reinforced concrete station name board installed in the mid-1920s by the London & North Eastern Railway which had absorbed the GNR under the terms of the Railway Grouping Act of 1921. Several other stations on the 'Queensbury Lines' network also had these name boards which were pioneered by William Marriott, engineer to the Midland & Great Northern Joint Railway, who established a concrete works at Melton Constable. A standard GNR cast iron notice, still in situ 43 years after the company disappeared, warns non-existent passengers to cross the line only by using the bridge. (*Arthur Hey*)

A panoramic view from the footbridge at Horton Park station in 1965, looking down the line towards Laisteridge Lane Bridge and Manchester Road Tunnel. It is difficult to imagine how busy the disused and overgrown platforms of this station used to be on match days at the adjacent football and cricket grounds, particularly between the 1890s and 1930s when thousands of supporters regularly arrived and departed by train. The Bradford Cricket, Athletic and Football Club had secured a lease on land at Horton in 1879 and the new cricket and rugby football grounds were opened a year later. Realising its potential, the GNR built a station across the road to cater for sports fans and also for visitors to Bradford Corporation's popular municipal park which had been laid off Horton Park Avenue in 1878. The new station greeted its first passengers on 23 October 1880 - nine days before its official opening - when several special trains were run in connection with an eagerly anticipated rugby match between Bradford and Halifax, which was won by the visitors. (*John Rothera*)

Horton Park was never intended to have goods facilities but sidings were laid in 1897 to accommodate empty coaches from special trains bringing visiting sports fans to Park Avenue. Until then, the stock had to be stabled at St. Dunstan's, Manchester Road or, occasionally, at Great Horton but this caused operational problems so a permanent solution was implemented. Seven sidings were laid on land near the station and, although specifically intended for passenger coaches awaiting their return journeys, empty goods wagons were also stabled there from time to time. Then, in the late 1950s, local merchants requested that the under-used sidings should be converted into a coal receiving depot. This was agreed by BR and track remodelling took place to create an efficient operation which initially required permanent staff and generated good revenue for the railway. By the time of this view in July 1965, the yard had been reduced to an unstaffed public delivery facility with four of the original seven sidings still in use. Further rationalisation saw two of these removed in 1967 to provide space for new coal hoppers and an expanded stacking area. *(John Rothera)*

A track level view at Great Horton looking back towards Horton Park a few days after track lifting at Thornton had started in April 1966. This explains why one of the lines is showing signs of recent use while the rest of the permanent way is very rusted. The stone parapets in the foreground are those of GNR Bridge No. 14 which carried the railway over Toby Lane. In the distance is Farnham Road bridge which was constructed of wrought iron girders with stone abutments. Seen on the left are the last few yards of a headshunt extended in 1903 to accommodate a private siding for the Horton Iron Works. The telegraph pole became part of local folklore in November 1956 when it prevented a runaway J50 tank locomotive from plunging into the street below. Unable to bring their train to a stop on greasy rails, the crew jumped out before the engine ran through the buffer stop and came to rest against the telegraph pole, an event which attracted the attention of the local newspaper. (John Rothera)

A fine panorama at the east end of Great Horton station looking out to the dense housing of Horton Grange and Manningham beyond, with the locally famous Lister's Mill standing like a sentinel on the horizon. The unusual cantilevered design of the signal box provided excellent visibility so signalling staff could supervise all operations in the yard and station area. The box was one of only three on the 'Queensbury Lines' built on a station platform – the other two being at Denholme and Ovenden, although the Ladies Waiting Room at Manchester Road was converted into a signal cabin after the station closed to passengers in December 1915. (*John Rothera*)

The signal post seen on the previous page provided the photographer with a high vantage point from which to record the infrastructure at the Bradford end of Great Horton station. Prominent on the right are eight double cell coal drops served by two sidings. Among the local merchants who continued to use these until their closure in 1965 was William Luty & Sons, who also operated from Clayton. The open wooden bodied wagons stabled there in April 1966 were waiting to be used for the recovery of redundant sleepers from track lifting operations at Thornton. The line on the extreme left is the former private siding to the Horton Iron Works which was taken over by Smith & Fawcett in 1917 and earned revenue for the railway until a few months before closure. *(John Rothera)*

Class 10 diesel shunter No. D3151 was temporarily transferred from Thornaby-on-Tees to Bradford for several months in 1963 so it could to assist in track-lifting operations between Halifax and Queensbury. Here, it is seen standing alongside the Up platform at Great Horton station awaiting permission to continue towards Clayton. As the line to Thornton and Cullingworth was still open for scheduled goods traffic at this time, paths for the extra track-lifting movements had to be carefully planned as the route was operated under 'one engine in steam' regulations which meant that only one train at a time could operate beyond Great Horton. The yellow contraption behind the brake van is a track machine produced for the LNER in 1929 by the Morris crane company. The Morris tracklayer - which was also adept at track-lifting - could deal with one panel every nine minutes and proved useful for removing redundant lines especially where clearances were tight, such as in tunnels. (D.J. Mitchell)

Following the announcement by British Railways in 1954 that it was proposing to withdraw passenger services between Keighley, Halifax and Bradford via Queensbury, a regular user observed that the infrastructure had 'long resembled a Victorian museum piece with dilapidated stations and pre-1923 equipment abounding.' His observations seem to be borne out here at Great Horton in 1965 where vintage hardware is still on show by the Beckside Road overbridge. Prominent is a Great Northern Railway Trespass Notice, dating from 1896, the original GNR 15 bridge number plate and a GNR cast iron signalling bracket. A Bradford Corporation water main runs over the line on a separate structure alongside the bridge and the lead from the goods yard can be seen re-joining the main line before the three-arch bridge carrying Old Corn Mill Lane over the railway. Following abandonment of the Down line beyond Great Horton in 1958, the Up line had been operated as a bi-directional section to Cullingworth under 'one engine in steam' regulations, as mentioned previously. To facilitate the new arrangements, a crossover was installed beyond the Old Corn Mill Lane bridge to allow the Down line to join the Up. Thornton became the end of the line in November 1963 after closure of Cullingworth and Wilsden but it too closed in June 1965, along with Great Horton. (*John Rothera*)

The elegant simplicity of the soot-stained stone-arch accommodation bridge at Paradise, between Great Horton and Clayton, contrasts starkly with the mismatched industrial buildings of Fields Printers beyond it. The tower and spire on the horizon belong to the church of St. John the Evangelist at Great Horton which was consecrated by the Right Rev. Bishop Ryan, Vicar of Bradford, on 10 March 1874 which, by coincidence, was the same day that the first sod of the Bradford and Thornton Railway was cut not far away in a field between Thornton Road and Legrams Lane. Wielding the commemorative spade that day was prominent mill owner Mr. A. B. Foster, of Queensbury, who had been at the forefront of the campaign for a railway connection linking Bradford, Queensbury and Halifax. This view dates from April 1965 when the line to Thornton was still open for a twice weekly coal train which ran on Tuesdays and Thursdays. *(John Rothera)*

Sod's Law – and one of those moments that photographers curse. Having carefully chosen his vantage point and waited patiently at the lineside just east of Clayton goods yard, John Rothera released the shutter at precisely the moment a gust of wind enveloped his subject in steam. The unidentified WD Austerity 2-8-0 locomotive and its brake van are heading on to the Pasture Lane embankment - a massive obstacle for the 1870s railway builders as it swallowed up thousands of tons of tipped material over many months before they were able to stablilise it. The engine is about to cross an accommodation bridge, known as Robertshaw's, which is now the location of Pentland Avenue, close to its junction with Pasture Lane. Behind it is the end of the Clayton Up refuge siding. A slightly shorter refuge siding was located next to the Down line behind the photographer. As can be clearly seen, only one of the former main lines is still in use, with the other heavily rusted and overgrown. This was the result of efforts to reduce maintenance costs, implemented in 1958 when the Down line beyond Great Horton was abandoned. All traffic then used the Up line in both directions, which required the guard to carry a single line staff from Great Horton signal box. (John Rothera)

With the remaining trackwork difficult to see under thick vegetation growth, a group of lads unaccustomed to seeing trains in their locality have decided to investigate the track-lifting activities at Clayton in May 1966. The locomotive in charge is Low Moor WD Austerity No. 90731 which was used frequently on these track-lifters over a period of several weeks. This view was captured near the site of the former Clayton passenger station and the two boys on the left are walking on one of the rails of the refuge siding seen in the previous photograph. Clayton had refuge sidings on each side of the main running lines which were used, when required, to hold freight trains so other traffic could pass but they were very rarely needed after the 1939-45 war. Clayton station was one of the 11 on the 'Queensbury Lines' closed to passengers after the last services on Saturday 21 May 1955. Its goods yard closed in April 1961, along with Denholme, but trains continued to pass through en route to Thornton until June 1965. (Ralph Wood)

Although it has slightly deteriorated, this very rare image was, at the time of writing, the earliest known colour photograph taken anywhere on the former GNR lines from Bradford to Halifax or Keighley. It shows the section down to the Queensbury end of Clayton Tunnel on a spring day in 1953, when the line was still open to passengers as well as heavy 'through' freight. On a normal weekday in 1953, between eight and twelve freight trains passed through Queensbury, either to or from Bradford, and double-heading was not uncommon. The neat appearance of the signalling and the permanent way in the early British Railways period contrasts sharply with the dire neglect which had taken over by time of the view on the opposite page. *(Tom Allatt)*

This is the scene on the Queensbury to Clayton Tunnel section in June 1965, just as the line was about to close. In the 12 years that had elapsed since the previous view, the passenger service had ceased, the 'through' routes to Keighley and Halifax had been abandoned, signalling had been removed and the line had been singled, with the remaining goods services to Thornton being operated on the former Up line. The spoil heap above the tunnel portal is from one of four shafts used in its construction. Two of these were retained for ventilation, whereas the others – including the one seen here - were filled when the tunnel was completed. (*John Rothera*)

This superb panorama shows how well the railway not only blended into the landscape but how it also enhanced it. Looking across the middle distance from the right, we see the wooden platelayers' cabin at the end of the Clayton Tunnel cutting, the iron occupation bridge, which is still a local landmark, the East Junction signal box, the station Booking Hall and the Keighley platforms curving away on to Queensbury Viaduct which had three arches, although one is obscured by trees. Next is the high stone arch bridge over Brow Lane and just beyond is another platelayers' cabin, converted from remains of the former North Junction signal box. This view is so different from the busy interchange station that Queensbury used to be in GNR days when three passenger trains would often arrive in quick succession from Bradford, Halifax and Keighley, triggering a mad dash between platforms for those wanting to make connections. (*John Rothera*)

The West Riding Tour DMU special train has arrived at Queensbury on Sunday, 6 September 1964 after a sedate run from Bradford Exchange which was scheduled to take 16 minutes for the 4 ½ mile journey. The East Junction signal box had been retained to manage the signalling for the whole of the 'Queensbury Triangle' when the other two signal boxes at the North and South junctions were taken out of use in 1924. It was rendered redundant when all 'through' freight from Bradford to Halifax and Keighley was withdrawn in May 1956 and stood for another ten years before it was demolished. (John M. Ryan)

Queensbury was originally served by a short-lived two-platform station which opened on 12 April 1879 and could only be reached by windswept footpaths from Scarlett Heights and Brow Lane. However, in response to intense pressure from influential local interests, the GNR's Directors approved construction of a new station with six platforms around a triangular layout - and a proper access road. It opened in September 1890 and a small goods yard was provided just over a year later. This 1965 view from the 'new' station is looking towards the site of the original platforms. The recess in the retaining wall between the East Junction signal box and the iron bridge accommodated one of the former waiting rooms. Access to four of the six new platforms was via staircases from the wrought iron footbridge seen here. Passengers could then reach the Halifax to Keighley platforms via a subway or on a boarded crossing. The Booking Office was situated on the upper level of the building on the right. The concrete name board still directs anyone arriving on the Bradford to Keighley platform to change for Halifax ten years after passenger services were withdrawn. (*Jack Wild*)

Great Northern Railway passenger services from Halifax were introduced to Holmfield on 5 December 1879 and through to Queensbury and Bradford ten days later. New stations were then opened at North Bridge on 25 March 1880 and at Ovenden on 2 June 1881. Completion of the line from Queensbury to Keighley in 1884 significantly increased demand which exposed the shortcomings of Halifax station and major alterations were carried out to cater for the extra traffic. These included a new high-level entrance from the bottom of Horton Street which required a substantial wrought iron bridge. Additional platforms for GNR trains were brought into use in October 1885 and the remainder of the station reconstruction was completed by the end of May 1886. Separate booking offices were provided, with the Lancashire & Yorkshire Railway occupying the left of the main station entrance and the Great Northern Railway on the right. This view of the station forecourt dates from 21 March 1967, by which time the old Halifax & Ovenden line had been closed to passengers for almost 12 years. All that remained of the route was a short stub to North Bridge which continued to be used for freight until April 1974. (*HMRS John Bateman Collection*)

Halifax was very much Lancashire & Yorkshire Railway territory whereas it was an outpost in the GNR empire. However, the two companies had developed a working relationship at Bradford where they shared Exchange station – the L&Y's original terminus in the city which was rebuilt and expanded to cater for GN trains. This spirit of co-operation continued at Halifax where they jointly owned and operated the line to Holmfield, although passenger services were provided only by the GNR. Freight was a different matter. Each company had separate goods yards at Halifax but they operated side by side from their own facilities elsewhere on the Joint line. This colourful scene overlooking the former GNR goods lines at the west end of Halifax station in 1956 shows ex-L&Y Aspinall freight engine No. 52399 in South Parade yard. The locomotive had entered service in 1900 and was withdrawn by Sowerby Bridge shed in March 1958. Alongside is one of a large class of 'Jinty' 0-6-0s, first introduced by the LMS in 1924 and based on a Midland Railway design of 1899. The two coaches are resplendent in the early British Railways crimson lake and cream livery introduced in 1949 and nicknamed 'blood and custard.' However, problems with staining on the cream upper panels led to this attractive livery being replaced by all over maroon. (*Arthur Wilson*)

From a similar vantage point used to take the photograph on the opposite page, we see an interloper from across the Pennines on 14 December 1957 in the shape of No. 49378 - a former London & North Western Railway 0-8-0 tender engine. These powerful and reliable heavy freight locomotives handled long distance goods trains for many years and lasted well into the British Railways era. This example emerged from Crewe Works in 1903 and was twice rebuilt during its long career – firstly by the LNWR and then, in 1938, by the LMS which fitted it with a higher pressure Belpaire boiler. 49378 was a Wigan Springs Branch engine throughout the 1950s and was finally withdrawn from there in November 1959 after a period in storage. Note the primitive conditions for the footplate crew, with only half of the cab covered. *(Arthur Wilson)*

Breakdown trains and re-railing equipment on the Halifax & Ovenden Joint line to Holmfield – and its associated High Level branch - were provided by the L&YR, which was the main player in the area. After the L&Y was absorbed into the LMS in 1923, the latter took on responsibility while the LNER, which had absorbed the GNR, continued as before. This late 1960s view shows the Healey Mills breakdown train, with Cowans Sheldon 45-ton steam crane DE330107 in its post-1959 British Railways red livery, taking centre stage at the east end of the former GNR Halifax South Parade goods depot. The crane, built in 1926, has survived and is now based on the North Yorkshire Moors Railway. The platforms closest to the crane were constructed around the original 1855 buildings during the upgrading of Halifax station in 1885/6 and were for GNR trains. The later additions to the station also included the approach bridge, water tank, booking offices and footbridges which can all be seen behind the original soot-stained building. (Jack Wild)

A panorama of the western end of Halifax station, with a departing Bradford to Stockport passenger train having just passed Halifax West signal box on its way towards Dryclough Junction in July 1965. Behind the signal box is the former GNR goods warehouse, with its facing side contoured to fit the tight space available at the time of construction. The train is about to pass the ex-L&YR goods depot at Shaw Syke with its unusual cream-coloured loading shed. This structure was the original roof which had covered the platforms at Halifax station until its rebuilding. It was then re-purposed for further use and spent far longer as a shed than it had as a roof. Halifax station has undergone a number of name changes over the years. The first was in 1890 when it was renamed 'Halifax Old' to distinguish it from the recently opened Halifax St. Pauls station on the High Level line from Holmfield. It took on the name 'Halifax Town' in 1951 and then, ten years later, went back to where it started, being named simply 'Halifax.' The Halifax Corporation Skircoat Road bus depot – formerly a tram shed - can be seen on the hill beyond the ex-L&YR goods warehouses. (*John Rothera*)

By the time of this view on 15 July 1972, the old GNR platforms at Halifax station had become weed-strewn and derelict but some of their 1950s BR North Eastern Region enamel signs were still in place, along with the much earlier gas lamp columns. The buildings and awnings on these platforms were demolished in July 1954, with the last lingering passenger services to Keighley and Bradford via Queensbury operating from the adjacent Platform 4. Track lifting around the abandoned platform and the adjacent goods loop lines was more recent but the tracks to the South Parade goods depot were still well used. Facilities in this busy former GNR yard were much improved after the LNER took over in 1923. Perhaps the most significant improvement in the day to day operation of the depot was the installation of an overhead travelling crane mounted on concrete supports which can be seen on the next page. Attached to the main warehouse is a canopy over three tracks which was added to allow goods to be transferred to or from road vehicles without getting wet. The Lilly Lane footbridge spans the lines at the entrance to the yard. The floodlights on the upper right mark the location of The Shay, Halifax Town Football Club's home ground since 1921. *(HMRS John Bateman Collection)*

The concrete structure of South Parade goods depot's electrically-powered overhead travelling crane is seen to good effect in this view from the Lilly Lane footbridge in 1972. The crane was situated alongside the run around loops (or wall sidings) provided so locomotives arriving with their trains could be quickly released for their next workings. The buffer stops at the ends of the loops were precisely 201 miles and 2 chains distance from GNR headquarters at London King's Cross, as recorded in the re-measurement of all the Great Northern lines in the Leeds District in April 1897. No evidence has ever been found to indicate whether the company actually placed a 201 milepost so close to the perimeter of the yard. (*HMRS John Bateman Collection*)

A fine broadside view of Fowler 2-6-4T No. 42394 with empty coaching stock at the east end of the South Parade goods yard. This passenger tank engine entered service in 1933 and went on to become the penultimate member of its class to be withdrawn. At the time of this view in 1965, the locomotive was allocated to Leeds Holbeck shed from where it was withdrawn in June 1966. The last of the Fowler tanks was No. 42410, of Huddersfield Hillhouse shed, which lasted another three months. One of the original pedestrian entrances to the 1855 Halifax station can just be seen above the coach in front of the gable end of the warehouses in Deal Street. Behind the locomotive is Halifax Goods Yard signal box, which controlled movements in and out of South Parade. (*Willowherb Publishing Collection*)

This excellent view from the east end of Halifax station shows the junction with the Halifax & Ovenden Joint line - with its 20 m.p.h. speed restriction - curving away on the left towards North Bridge Viaduct. The approaching Metropolitan Cammell DMU has just emerged from Beacon Hill Tunnel on the former L&YR main line from Low Moor. Of particular interest is the rare L&YR and GNR Joint Railways cast iron trespass notice at the end of the platform. Relevant information on the notice has been picked out in white but the original company names have been painted over. Few of these notices have survived so they are now eagerly sought after by railwayana collectors and command high prices. This example is an L&YR casting which was the type used at Halifax and on the H&O. Even rarer GNR-style Joint notices were erected on the Halifax High Level line, as will be seen later. *(Geoff Brown)*

The industrial environment around Halifax is well illustrated in this fascinating view, looking across to the North Bridge goods yard in 1964. Prominent are Halifax Corporation's gas and electricity works which both relied on coal delivered by the railway. This continuing requirement ensured that the short section of line between Halifax and North Bridge, which had been the first part of the 'Queensbury Lines' network to open in August 1874, was the last fragment to survive. The end finally came in April 1974, just four months short of a century of service. A BR Class 03 diesel shunter, out stationed from Bradford Hammerton Street, can be seen at the end of the viaduct near North Bridge South signal box. This local 'pilot' loco was also used to shunt South Parade and Shaw Syke yards. Railway business at North Bridge still appears to be healthy at this time and it is interesting to note that a spare siding on the right is being used to store empty passenger coaches. (*Jan Rapacz Collection*)

An evocative Halifax street scene from July 1965 at a location that is totally unrecognisable today due to the wholesale clearance of properties and the building of the Burdock flyover and its approach roads. The photographer is looking down New Bank towards North Bridge and Dean Clough. The Great Northern Hotel was just a stone's throw from the former North Bridge passenger station and was a tangible reminder of the railway heritage in that part of Halifax until it was swept away in the late 1960s. The hotel was located on the corner of Range Bank, with the Pineapple Hotel opposite. Both hotels carry advertising for the famous 'Cock o' the North' ales brewed locally by Richard Whitaker & Sons. Production at Whitaker's Corporation Street brewery, visible in the background, ceased in 1969 after it was taken over by Whitbread. The approaching bus is a Weymann-bodied Leyland Titan in the distinctive Halifax Corporation livery. It is following an Albion lorry operated by Harrison and Page Ltd., of Bradford, which is making slow progress up New Bank with its heavy load of wool bales. A second Halifax motor bus is about to turn into Haley Hill towards Queensbury. (*John Rothera*)

Both the L&YR and the GNR shared a large two-storey goods warehouse at North Bridge but their operations were kept separate. Each company had its own office and two lines served by four small cranes for loading and unloading inside the building. The smaller opening into the warehouse was for railway wagons while the larger opening next to it provided access for both road and rail vehicles. This enabled the transhipment of merchandise to be completed much faster. Part of the interior loading stage can just be seen in the doorway behind the 16-ton steel mineral wagon basking in the sun as it waits to be unloaded on 15 July 1972. Alongside the warehouse, another of these ubiquitous wagons stands in the shade. Originally developed to the specification of the Ministry of Transport during the 1939-45 war, these wagons had two side drop doors and one end door. The white diagonal stripe indicates the position of the end door. More than 300,000 of this type were eventually built and they became BR's standard mineral wagon which could be seen throughout the network. (*HMRS John Bateman Collection*)

One of the main objectives of the Halifax & Ovenden Railway was to establish a goods depot at North Bridge to serve the local manufacturing district and to relieve pressure around Halifax station. It was an important yard which had 14 cranes of various sizes, rail and road weighbridges, nine coal offices, a wagon repair shed, cart sheds and horse stables. The L&YR and its successor, the LMS, and the GNR and its successor, the LNER, both worked goods and coal over the H&O, but the L&Y/LMS had no involvement with the passenger traffic as it ran beyond the Joint line at Holmfield and on to GNR/LNER territory. The iconic North Bridge stands against the industrial backdrop on a snowy day in March 1969 as a Hebble bus crosses the railway heading for the town centre. The bridge, with its twin 160 ft. spans, was constructed in cast and wrought iron and opened in 1871. The elliptical design allowed maximum clearance for the railway under one span while the Hebble Brook, a road and part of the North Bridge Dye Works were accommodated beneath the other. After closure of the railway beyond North Bridge in 1960, the main line was truncated and a coal stacking area was laid for the merchants still receiving their supplies by rail. Two mineral wagons can be seen near the stacking area under the bridge. (*Jack Wild*)

Late afternoon sun highlights the grimy appearance of ex-L&YR Aspinall 0-6-0 locomotive No. 52400 as it rests between shunting duties at North Bridge on 5 March 1960. This vintage engine, which was new in 1900, was a regular visitor to North Bridge yard for many years, having been transferred to Sowerby Bridge shed in the 1940s. But its time was running out and it was withdrawn eight months later, then scrapped. The wagons behind the engine to the right were waiting be shunted into the Halifax Corporation Gas Works siding to be emptied into a covered coal bunker to feed the retorts producing town gas. Although North Bridge goods yard handled a wide variety of merchandise in its heyday, its principal traffic was always coal. For a number of years, however, it was also an important railhead for moving dressed stone brought down from quarries at Southowram. Three cranes were provided to load the stone into railway wagons for onward shipment to customers all over the country. (*Arthur Wilson*)

A few days after the last trainloads of coal had been delivered to Holmfield - then to Pellon and St. Paul's on the Halifax High Level branch - Sowerby Bridge shed dispatched Newton Heath's 'Black Five,' No. 45339, to clear the empty wagons from the three yards. The locomotive and its ex-Midland Railway brake van are seen here under the faded sign for the North Bridge Wood Works before making the final trip on 29 June 1960. The line beyond North Bridge was then closed and did not see another train for 2½ years when the first of the track-lifters ran. The passenger station platforms and buildings - closed in 1955 - had been recently demolished to make way for a coal stacking area. Some track rationalisation had also taken place to extend the stacking space, with one of the main lines and the entry into North Bridge goods yard from the Ovenden direction having been lifted. This had left just a single line to connect with the double track beyond – a short-lived requirement as the route was about to close. (J.C.W. Halliday)

The fireman and guard for the last train to Holmfield, Pellon and St. Paul's on 29 June 1960 have joined local railway management to discuss the state of the track at the crossover point where the line from Ovenden had been singled. They are standing below the wrought iron pedestrian footbridge carrying the unusually named 'Stony Battery' footpath over the line. This bridge, which still stands, was rebuilt with a new superstructure of steel girders and a concrete floor in 1936. It originally had a timber deck. The 403-yards long Old Lane Tunnel can be seen beyond. Also in view on the right is a private siding holding several wagons. This fell away to dive under the main line in a short, sharply curved tunnel before entering Crossley's Dean Clough Mills complex just in front of the tunnel portal. *(J.C.W. Halliday)*

Demolition of the lines to the south of Queensbury Tunnel commenced in March 1963 following completion of track recovery on the Halifax High Level line, which had begun in 1962. By the time of this view many months later, the operation had reached North Bridge where track panels were being lifted with the assistance of WD Austerity 2-8-0 No. 90113 and a rail-mounted crane. The immense retaining walls seen here were among the many challenges the railway contractors had to overcome to forge a railway through the heavily industrialised landscape to the north of Halifax. Work began in 1866 but had to be suspended a year later as the costs spiralled, forcing the promoters to seek Parliamentary approval to double their capital. The first goods finally started running to North Bridge on 17 August 1874. Lifting of the old H&O line in 1963 stopped at North Bridge where a single line was retained to Halifax so the goods yard could continue to be served. It finally closed on 1 April 1974. *(D.J. Mitchell)*

On 30 March 1963, an unidentified WD Austerity locomotive coasts down the gradient towards North Bridge and Halifax, having just emerged from Lee Bank Tunnel with a track-lifting train from the Holmfield area, while a pair of Halifax Corporation's AEC Regent III buses go about their duties. At 267 yards long, Lee Bank was one of the more modest tunnels on the 'Queensbury Lines' network. Colourful advertising hoardings of the period contrast with their drab industrial surroundings. Lee Bank cotton mill can be seen adjacent to the railway and the Old Lane woollen mill is in the distance. The truncated remains of the chimney on the right belonged to the Old Lane Dyeworks. The tunnel portal and railway formation at this location were swept away by road improvements when the old Lee Bank was replaced by a dual carriageway. (*D.J. Mitchell*)

The Halifax platform at Ovenden still looks well-kept and ready for service even though the station had been closed to passengers five years previously. The most obvious clue to the status of the station is the encroaching vegetation on the platform on the left which, until 1955, had served passengers for Holmfield and beyond. Although Ovenden never had any goods facilities or sidings, a signal box was provided on this platform until the early 1920s when it was closed and removed. The platform was then reconstructed. Remarkably, the wooden station buildings and the stone-built Station Master's House, seen here on the right, were still intact at the time of writing in 2020. Another survivor is the stone bridge in the distance which carries Old Lane over what is left of the railway formation. This view was taken from the brake van of the last goods train to run through the station on 29 June 1960. It was conveying empty wagons collected from the yards at Halifax St Paul's, Pellon and Holmfield which had closed a couple of days earlier. (*J.C.W. Halliday*)

Recovery of redundant track from the main lines and goods yards on the High Level and Halifax & Ovenden lines was a major operation spread over about a year which required at least one Class 8 steam locomotive in attendance every day. WD Austerity locomotives from Sowerby Bridge shed were the usual motive power as they had sufficient braking strength to control heavy trains of recovered track panels on the falling gradient towards Halifax. The British Railways District Operating Department also borrowed a 350 horsepower Blackstone-engined Class 10 diesel shunter from Thornaby-on-Tees shed to support the work. This locomotive – D3151 – was seen earlier at Great Horton. It was mainly used to shunt wagons and haul the recovery crane and other rail-borne equipment to where they were needed and it proved reliable throughout the duration of the contract. It is seen here emitting an impressive trail of exhaust 'clag' at Churn Milk Lane, between Holmfield and Ovenden, with a twin-jib crane in tow in April 1963. *(D.J. Mitchell)*

From a different vantage point, but at the same location featured on the opposite page, WD Austerity No. 90329 is seen a few weeks later as it ploughs through the grass towards Holmfield to resume track-lifting duties on the only line still in situ. This Sowerby Bridge engine was a regular on these duties until their completion. It was then transferred to Wakefield where it saw another two years of service before being withdrawn in 1965. The building alongside the railway is part of an engineering works, founded in 1847, which had a workforce of 800 in its late 19th century heyday. (D.J. Mitchell)

Demolition works are underway at Holmfield as WD Austerity No. 90412 stands between the roofless goods shed and the derelict signal box on 22 March 1963. It had just returned from a reconnaissance trip through Queensbury Tunnel to test track condition and confirm that there were no obstacles on the line prior to the start of track lifting. Holmfield gained importance as a railway junction when the Halifax High Level Railway - another GNR & LYR Joint undertaking - was opened in September 1890.

Originally intended to provide a line to the upper part of Halifax where it would connect with a proposed extension of the Hull and Barnsley Railway, this was never achieved and the High Level route terminated just over three miles from Holmfield. The new HHLR connection increased the complexity of signalling at Holmfield so, a month before the new branch opened for traffic, the signal box was fitted with a 70-lever Saxby & Farmer frame. (*D.J. Mitchell*)

A rather grim scene at Holmfield in March 1960 with the junction of the High Level line to Halifax St. Paul's diverging to the right near the signal box. This short branch was heavily engineered and expensive to build. As well as 16 bridges, it required a half mile long tunnel and a stone 10-arch viaduct at Wheatley, where a small goods yard was laid. In spite of the overwhelming sense of abandonment, the shiny rails indicate that there was still some traffic at the time of this view. Holmfield's importance as a junction was reinforced when the Great Northern Railway Company built an engine shed there to house and maintain locomotives required to operate the High Level branch and other local duties. Although the branch closed to passengers at the end of 1916, freight traffic remained heavy and the loco shed continued in service until 1933 when Sowerby Bridge took on responsibility for providing motive power for the H&O and HHL lines. (*Jack Wild*)

The young train spotter on the disused Pellon station platform would not have had anything else to write down in his notebook as this would be the only working of the day on the High Level line in the last week of operation in June 1960. 'Black Five' No. 45339 – which would return a few days later to collect the last empty wagons from the branch – draws a short rake of open wooden planked wagons from the two-storey goods shed. Three 'short' bolster wagons laden with steel sections await unloading in the sidings behind the locomotive while a solitary mineral wagon occupies the coal drops siding at the far end of the goods yard. Pellon was the principal freight depot on the High Level line and a private siding connection was provided for James Chalmers, timber merchants, who were still operating from the same location at the time of writing. Another short line branched off the Chalmers siding to serve a local petroleum and oil supplier. These sidings were laid in 1891 and 1898 respectively. The Pellon yard site has largely disappeared under various industrial units and a new road - aptly called High Level Way. The line to Halifax St. Pauls can be seen curving away to the right of the goods shed towards Battinson Road bridge, with the Ryburne woollen mill beyond. (J.C.W. Halliday)

A delightful view from the end of the abandoned island platform at Halifax St. Paul's station, looking back towards the Hopwood Lane bridge and Pellon, on 30 April 1960. The Halifax High Level & North & South Junction Railway Company - to give its full title – set out with big ideas to be part of a new through route to the East Coast by connecting with an extension of the Hull & Barnsley Railway but it ended up as nothing more than a short branch terminating in the King Cross district of Halifax. However, the terminus station at St Paul's was well appointed. It had a 45ft. turntable, a coal stage and other facilities for engine servicing as well as a fan of five goods sidings.

The engine turntable was situated just behind the creosoted wooden platelayer's cabin with the blue door. A very rare GNR Joint Railways trespass notice can be seen at the end of the platform. These notices, with the GNR name preceding the L&YR, were only used on the HHLR with the L&Y type, seen on Page 57, used on the H&O line. St. Paul's was short-lived as a passenger station, closing after only 26 years in business, but its goods depot fared much better with 70 years of service to its credit. It was closed two months after this photo was taken. (Arthur Wilson)

Another view of the St. Paul's terminus station and goods yard taken on the same day as the previous photograph but looking the other way. Although the platform awnings had been removed some years earlier, most of the station fabric remained intact as some of the offices continued to be used by railway staff and still featured signage for the separate goods offices of the LNER and the LMS which had superseded the GNR and L&YR in 1923. St. Paul's station closed to passengers at the end of 1916 but was reopened for occasional special excursions well into the 1950s. But by the time of this view, an air of decay pervaded the scene with a few coal wagons in the goods yard overseen by the dilapidated glazed roof over the small station concourse. Just visible in the haze on the horizon above the station is the top of the Wainhouse Tower, a well-known local landmark which was originally intended as a chimney for the local dye works of John Edward Wainhouse. It was never used as such and stands as an impressive folly from a bygone age. (*Arthur Wilson*)

Back at Holmfield, 'Black Five' No. 45339 assembles the very last train of wagons from the High Level yards with those collected from Holmfield on 29 June 1960, two days after closure of the line beyond North Bridge to normal traffic. The engine is attracting the interest of some young onlookers as preparations are made to depart for Halifax from the Up platform. This platform had been extended in 1890 to accommodate a bay for the new High Level line passenger services. Note that the station footbridge has steps up to the landing from both sides whereas, on the Down platform, only a single-sided staircase was provided. (*Gavin Morrison*)

A general track level view of Holmfield station looking towards Queensbury on a bright but very cold Friday, 28 December 1962. With frost still clinging to the redundant track, the only warm place in the vicinity appears to be the interior of the brake van on the right, judging by the smoke being emitted from the stove chimney. It is stabled in the cattle dock siding, having been involved in track lifting operations on the High Level line which had resumed following the Christmas break. The diamond crossover track in the foreground eased the task of shunting the various sidings on the east side of the main running lines. (*Arthur Wilson*)

WD Austerity No. 90310 appears to have gone to grass as it heads back to Holmfield through Strines cutting after a visit to Queensbury Tunnel where track-lifting was well advanced in May 1963. The Up line had already been lifted several weeks previously and nature was quickly covering the scar. The locomotive has just passed under a stone arch aqueduct carrying Strines Beck over the railway. The beck had to be diverted during construction and the aqueduct was 34 feet high with a 26 ft. span. Strines cutting was a monumental achievement by the railway navvies who drove it through solid rock using little more than primitive hand tools and dynamite. It continued for more than half a mile to Queensbury Tunnel at a depth of up to 60 feet and was among the greatest challenges to be overcome to complete the line from Halifax to Queensbury. (D.J. Mitchell)

It is late March 1963 and both lines through Strines cutting are still in situ as the photographer uses the parapet of the Strines Beck Aqueduct to capture this high level view of diesel shunter D3151 which has just emerged from Queensbury Tunnel with a track-lifting train. The two loaded wagons would be detached at Holmfield to await a WD Class 8 steam locomotive to take them to Halifax, along with others already stabled in the yard. The small diesel had insufficient braking power to handle such heavy trains on the steep falling gradient to Halifax so would return whence it came with empty wagons to be loaded with more redundant track. Queensbury Tunnel was another triumph of Victorian engineering. It was 2,501 yards long and 379 feet underground at its deepest point. When opened on 31 July 1878, it was the second longest railway tunnel in the country. After the Queensbury to Holmfield section closed to traffic in 1956, a track panel was removed from both lines in Strines cutting and buffer stops were installed to block the route. The lines had to be fully reinstated seven years later to enable the track-lifting operations to take place. D3151 was built at Darlington Works in 1955 but lasted a mere 12 years in service, having been declared surplus to requirements due to loss of traffic and the closure of many goods yards. It was scrapped in April 1968. *(D.J. Mitchell)*

The abandoned Bradford to Halifax platform at Queensbury station on 22 April 1963 finds Mirfield's WD Austerity No. 90333 at the head of a couple of redundant passenger coaches being used as tool vans in connection with the track-lifting operations in Queensbury Tunnel. The tool vans were returned to Bradford when the day's work was completed as it was no longer possible to reach Halifax from Queensbury by this date. This also meant that the locomotive was provided by Low Moor rather than Sowerby Bridge shed. The siding in the foreground is one of two constructed at Queensbury station early in 1892 to handle goods traffic. These were laid following pressure from the local wool magnate, John Foster, who owned the famous Black Dyke Mills – the biggest employer in the district. The two sidings could accommodate a maximum of 28 wagons and were complimented by a weigh office and a small loading dock. There was never any covered accommodation. The sidings closed in November 1963 but remained in situ until 1966 when track was lifted from all three sides of Queensbury station. The Halifax to Keighley section of the Queensbury triangle runs across the background of this view, just beyond the train. (D.J. Mitchell)

Long after passenger trains stopped calling, the seemingly indestructible concrete name board on the Bradford-Halifax platform at Queensbury still announces that a change is required to get to Keighley. Looking towards the station buildings and the line towards Clayton Tunnel, the track has almost vanished under vegetation. It is a very depressing scene. The extent of the compact goods yard is visible behind the station name board. A plan by Foster's to provide a connection between these railway sidings and an inclined tramway up to Queensbury was abandoned after stone abutments were built half way up Station Road. The remains of these can still be seen. The proposed tramway would have enabled loaded wagons to be hauled to the township of Queensbury at the top of the hill using a stationary winding engine. This failure was exacerbated when an alternative scheme was put forward by the GNR to expand the goods yard to five sidings and build a warehouse to accommodate eight wagons required for the Fosters' mill traffic. This too did not proceed even though the required land had been secured by the GNR in 1899. (*Jack Wild*)

Resuming our journey on the Bradford and Thornton line, we renew acquaintance with the RCTS Special DMU during its 20-minute stop at Queensbury on 6 September 1964. This unusual view was taken from the station footbridge looking back towards East junction. The small brick building opposite the signal box is a lamp hut constructed on the site of the Bradford platform of the original 1879 Queensbury station, referred to on Page 48. *(Geoff Brown)*

On the Bradford to Thornton leg of the RCTS West Riding Tour, the leading two coaches, seen here, were formed of a Metropolitan Cammell diesel multiple unit twin set (cars 51429 and 51499), with a three-car BRCW 'Calder Valley' formation at the rear. This view was taken from the Bradford-Keighley platform at Queensbury which had been disused since the withdrawal of passenger services nine years earlier. As stated previously, all remaining goods traffic to and from Thornton used the Up line after the Down was taken out of use in 1958 to save on maintenance costs. This meant that the train had to use the Keighley to Bradford platform even though it was heading in the opposite direction. (Geoff Brown)

Greeting passengers at Queensbury was a cow on the platform which seemed to enjoy the unexpected attention. After an extended stop to allow photographers to record the visit for posterity, the train continued to Thornton. This was the last time any of the Queensbury station platforms was used by passengers as the DMU ran through without stopping on the return journey. The leading car is showing 'Keighley' on its destination panel, a hint of what might have been on the Queensbury line had it not been for the bloody-mindedness of the British Railways hierarchy in the mid-1950s. Their response to requests by local people and politicians to try the new cheaper-to-run diesel units on the line instead of just closing all the stations to passengers without any real thought for possible alternatives was fobbed with silly excuses which did not add up. But those were times of less scrutiny on public officials and they got away with it. *(J.C.W. Halliday)*

This epitome of 'faded glory' (and the cover photograph for this book) shows a work weary B1, No. 61016 *Inyala*, crossing Queensbury Viaduct with two coal empties from Thornton to Laisterdyke on the glorious afternoon of Monday, 24 August 1964 – two weeks before the RCTS Special seen on the previous pages. This was the last summer of steam operation on the Bradford and Thornton route and loadings had declined steeply as a result of BR's policy of driving away customers by no longer providing support for certain traffic flows on lines it wanted to close. The iron brackets on the viaduct had held part of the Bradford to Keighley platform which was removed in 1957, two years after closure of the station. *(Howard Malham)*

The Queensbury cow was not the only unexpected animal encounter on the RCTS West Riding Tour of 6 September 1964. As the DMU approached the Headley Lane bridge, half a mile from Thornton, the driver spotted a white goat on the railway embankment and brought the train to a stand. The driver, guard and a railway manager travelling with the train, all alighted to investigate and are seen here checking the welfare of the goat and reminding the owner that this was still an operational railway and that his livestock should not be anywhere near the running lines, even though Sunday operations had been virtually unknown since the end of 1938. The train then continued on its way, arriving at Thornton a few minutes late. (J.C.W. Halliday)

Following closure to passengers in May 1955, freight traffic at some yards on the 'Queensbury Lines' increased, largely thanks to the efforts of local staff. One such success story was at Thornton where the Station Master, Bernard Whitaker, had remained in post after passenger services ended. He then became responsible for all goods depots between Horton Park and Cullingworth and set about trying to secure new business for the railway. As a result, Thornton became a railhead distribution centre in 1958, with its own fleet of road vehicles and increased staffing. Deliveries of farm livestock feeds, timber and other commodities from Thornton goods depot covered a wide area and included customers in Calderdale in the south and the Aire Valley to the north. These arrangements remained in place until the British Railways regional management lost interest and stopped the business as they had the depot on their hit-list for closure. However, between 1958 and 1963, Thornton yard was the busiest it had been for years and, on some days, there was hardly any siding space to accommodate the trainloads of goods arriving every weekday. This view of the 'middle sidings' in Thornton yard in the winter of 1963, shows loaded wagons awaiting attention and also rake of empties awaiting collection. Beyond the yard, the majestic 20-arch Thornton Viaduct curves away towards Headley and Queensbury. (D.J. Mitchell)

It all started to go downhill during 1964 when BR pulled out of all but the coal business and, by the end of that year, Thornton had become an unstaffed public delivery siding served by two trains a week conveying a few wagonloads of coal for the seven local merchants still relying on rail deliveries. Before the downturn had taken a hold, WD Austerity No. 90351 rests in Thornton yard during shunting duties after bringing in the morning freight from Laisterdyke in March 1963. The yard finally closed during the last week of June in 1965, leaving the coal merchants – some of whom had been railway customers at Thornton for more than 50 years - to travel elsewhere for their supplies. Great Horton yard closed on the same day. Total revenue generated by the two depots in the previous year had amounted to £13,086, which is almost £200,000 at today's values. British Railways stated that closing them would save just over £6,000 a year (£87,000 today) in staff and maintenance costs. That seems to have been an inflated estimate to satisfy accountants as there had been virtually no expenditure on maintenance beyond Horton Junction for years and both depots were unstaffed. The only staff costs in 1965 related to train crew who worked the infrequent coal trips as part of their duties at City Road. *(D.J. Mitchell)*

With storm clouds building, redundant track materials recovered from the Wilsden area are being lifted from wagons on the 'Long Dock' siding in Thornton goods yard in August 1964. The line beyond Thornton had been abandoned after withdrawal of goods services at Cullingworth and Wilsden in November 1963 and recovery of track began in May 1964. The locomotive and crew allocated to the daily Laisterdyke to Thornton trip freight then had to go up to wherever the demolition gang had reached with empty wagons for loading and also to bring back loaded wagons to Thornton where track panels and other material were sorted and separated into scrap metal and wood. This operation continued until late October 1964 when the track had been cut back to a point near Wellhead Tunnel, half a mile north of Thornton. The contractor for the job was Coventry-based T.W. Ward Ltd. whose crane can be seen piling up track panels lifted the previous day. Lack of investment over a long period meant that some of the permanent way in goods yards on the Queensbury lines had been obsolete for years. Dozens of iron railchairs taken from sleepers recovered from sidings at Cullingworth and Wilsden were marked 'GNR' and dated from between 1900 and 1910. (D.J. Mitchell)

The RCTS West Riding Tour Special was the first passenger train at Thornton since 1955 and it would be the last. The station had been demolished in June and July 1963, leaving a scene of appalling dereliction. No effort whatsoever was made by BR's contractors to tidy up or make the site safe. Instead, the island platform was left strewn with rubble, glass and twisted gas pipes. Notwithstanding, the DMU driver brought his train to stand in what remained of the platform and passengers were allowed to disembark and pick their way around mess. Between 1952 and 1954, Thornton station had won four awards for its neatness and the quality of its platform garden. What a rapid and a spectacular fall from grace the next ten years had wrought upon it. The three-car BRCW unit comprising cars E51848, 59712 and 51828, would lead the train out of Thornton on the next leg of its tour which involved a trip down the freight-only City Road branch from Horton Junction, where it was seen on Page 24. *(J.C.W. Halliday)*

This is history being made – the precise moment at just after 1120 a.m. on Sunday, 6 September 1964 when the last ever passenger train to depart from Thornton station slowly pulled away from the platform. The mood of the moment has been captured perfectly by the man looking out of the window of the last coach who appears to be lost in his own wistful thoughts. *(J.C.W. Halliday)*

Goods trains to Wilsden and Cullingworth were timetabled to run as required during 1963 - their last year of operation. In practice, they tended to run to Wilsden on most weekdays as demand for coal by local merchants remained substantial. Traffic to Cullingworth was more unpredictable but the yard there was usually served at least three times a week. One such train is seen rounding the curve under the high arch of the Thornton Road bridge and on towards Wellhead Tunnel in March 1963. The large building with the wide curving roof was part of the Thornton Fireclay Works which made high quality pipes and retorts for the gas industry, using fireclay mined on site. From 1920, it had its own half mile long private siding which was used to send out wagonloads of its products to customers all over the country. Use of the siding declined through the 1940s and it had fallen into disuse by 1954. However, it was not officially closed until 18 September 1957. *(R.L. Mitchell)*

Supposedly secret testing of the effects of diesel fumes compared to smoke from a steam locomotive in a confined space led to Lees Moor Tunnel on the closed section between Cullingworth and Ingrow being 'reopened' for experiments in December 1957 and January 1958. The line had closed in May 1956 when all 'through' freight from Laisterdyke and Halifax to Keighley was re-routed via Shipley (Windhill). Two brand new English Electric Type 1 diesel locomotives, D8010/11, were brought up from Devon's Road depot in London to generate the fumes while, bizarrely, the only 'local' steam locomotive apparently available for the duration of the tests was Leeds Neville Hill's A3 Pacific, No. 60081 Shotover – an engine more accustomed to hauling prestigious expresses on the East Coast main line than slumming it in a disused tunnel on a closed line in the middle of nowhere. News that something very unusual was happening soon spread and several photographers recorded Shotover as it made its daily trips to and from Lees Moor. However, this exceedingly rare view of the locomotive heading through Denholme on its way back to Bradford is the only known colour image of what was a remarkable, albeit short lived, chapter in the history of the line. A colour photograph of the two diesels on the line has yet to emerge. (John Carter)

Stanier 'Black Five' locomotives were unusual visitors but on 20 March 1963, No. 44951 was provided by Low Moor shed in lieu of the usual WD Austerity 2-8-0 to work the morning Laisterdyke to Cullingworth trip. Having completed its duties at Thornton, it is seen shunting Wilsden coal yard before continuing on to Cullingworth. Although it was one of the smaller depots on the route, Wilsden generated a lot of business, even in the last few months before it was closed in November 1963. For example, on Friday 18 October 1963, three weeks before the last coal was delivered by rail, Wilsden yard held 13 loaded wagons and nine empties were taken away to make space for more arrivals the following week. British Railways had first raised the prospect of closing Wilsden coal yard in 1958 but backed off after political pressure and angry complaints from customers which were reported in the local media. That stay of execution was to last for five years. *(D.J. Mitchell)*

The Great Northern Railway's lines linking Bradford, Halifax and Keighley via Queensbury, and their associated short branches, made up a total distance of only 21 miles. But within that local network, the Victorian builders had to overcome immense engineering challenges and they left us with some of most iconic railway structures anywhere in the country. Two of these are the magnificent viaducts at Thornton and here at Hewenden, near Cullingworth. Both of these Grade 2 Listed Buildings - just over three miles apart - are now in the custodianship of the sustainable transport charity SUSTRANS and form part of the Great Northern Railway Trail which attracts thousands of visitors every year. Hewenden Viaduct has 17 arches, each of

50 feet span, and was built from locally quarried stone. It stands on foundations sunk 60 feet through unstable ground. In total, the 'Queensbury Lines' system had seven viaducts, 17 tunnels – including one of the longest in the country at Queensbury – well over 100 bridges, numerous culverts and a series of deep cuttings and high embankments. It is no coincidence that the main contractors were Messers Benton & Woodiwiss who had previous experience of driving railways through hostile landscapes. They had also built the highest part of the Settle-Carlisle line – dubbed England's most spectacular railway. In terms of engineering achievement, the 'Queensbury Lines' ran it close, albeit on a smaller scale. (Robert Anderson)

Track-lifting on the Thornton to Cullingworth line had reached Hewenden Viaduct where the Down line had already disappeared by the time of this view on 20 August 1964. In attendance is Low Moor B1 No. 61016 *Inyala* which had worked the Thornton trip freight earlier in the day. The locomotive - a regular performer on these duties at the time - had then been required to take empty wagons to Wilsden in connection with the track recovery operations and also collect wagons loaded with redundant materials. These were hauled back to Thornton where they were left in the goods yard for sorting. The rails, chairs and other metal fixings were graded for onward shipment to a scrap firm in South Yorkshire, as seen on Page 88, while the recovered wooden sleepers were re-loaded into separate wagons for disposal. This operation continued from late May 1964, when the first siding was lifted in Cullingworth yard, until late October when the line was cut back to just north of Thornton. *(Gavin Morrison)*

An interested observer gives a sense of scale to this view of a bogie bolster wagon awaiting loading just east of Cullingworth Viaduct in June 1964 as track-lifting takes place a quarter of a mile away, behind the photographer. Less than 18 months earlier, regular trainloads of bogie bolsters loaded with pre-cast concrete beams left the private siding of the nearby 'Grippon' works of George Greenwood & Sons. This connection, which was laid in 1885 to serve a stone quarry, curved away from the heavily overgrown track on the right. The beams were used for motorway bridge building and earned substantial and profitable revenue for the railway between 1959 and early 1963 when British Railways informed the customer that it was no longer willing to cater for the traffic. The siding closed on 1 February 1963 and, just over nine months later, the line from Thornton to Cullingworth was also axed. As can be seen in the distance, the Up line had been slewed on to the Down to improve access to the private siding when the concrete traffic began in 1959. *(John Rothera)*

The announcement by British Railways in early October 1963 that the last loaded freight train to Cullingworth would run on Friday 8 November - three days ahead of the official closure date - gave the remaining customers less than five weeks to start making alternative arrangements for their deliveries. Unlike Wilsden, which had become exclusively a coal depot in its last year of operation, Cullingworth had continued to receive other goods and merchandise as well as coal, including livestock feeds, farm machinery and bricks for a building materials supplier. However, loadings tended to be light in the months leading up to closure and there were some days when the daily freight from Laisterdyke terminated either at Thornton or Wilsden. 'Black Five' No. 44951, seen earlier at Wilsden, has arrived at Cullingworth on 20 March 1963 where it is seen in the yard after depositing one wagonload of bricks and three wagons of coal. There were no empties to take out on this day so the engine returned with just its brake van. (D.J. Mitchell)

After closure to passengers in May 1955, Cullingworth was one of several stations on the line which continued to see service as BR honoured bookings for summer holiday excursions to seaside resorts such as Blackpool and Morecambe. There was also a special train to Belle Vue (Manchester) for visitors to the famous Zoological Gardens which ran on 3 September 1955. Thereafter, all the stations were left to fall into disrepair. This is Cullingworth station in May 1964, with its impressive but redundant wrought iron footbridge still standing proud over the rusted lines. Within two months, the whole site would be cleared. A quarter mile stretch of the Up line into the Bradford and Halifax platform had been relaid with concrete sleepers in 1950. The last of these can be seen just before the connection into the goods yard. A section near Whins Wood on the closed section between Lees Moor Tunnel and Ingrow was also laid with concrete sleepers and, on 18 July 1957, the durability of these was severely tested when a G5 tank engine, No. 67338, and its motley rake of redundant stock were deliberately derailed over them to see what would happen. The damaged line was then lifted the following year, thereby severing the link with Cullingworth. (John Rothera)

The imprint of the Down line about ¾ mile north of Cullingworth can be seen as the track bed curves away towards the Ellar Carr occupation bridge (GNR No. 55) which still carries a public footpath over the old railway formation. This section, closed in 1956, had been brought back into use in December 1957/January 1958 for the tests in Lees Moor Tunnel, referred to on Page 92. Contractors moved in to lift the track in the autumn of 1958. This evocative view dates from the following summer so new vegetation had yet to take a firm hold. *(M. Teale)*

After Bridge 55, the line curved into a deep cutting on the approach to Lees Moor Tunnel - a location well off the beaten track so rarely visited by photographers. This view, taken after the one on the previous page in June 1959, shows the south entrance to the tunnel. At 1,533 yards, Lees Moor was the longest tunnel between Bradford and Keighley but 968 yards shorter than Queensbury Tunnel on the line from Halifax. It was built on a long curve with a steep gradient, had no ventilation shafts and was very wet. This meant that heavy trains struggling for traction in the Cullingworth direction could take ten minutes to clear the tunnel, leaving their crews gasping for oxygen. The wooden platelayers' hut on the right was typical of the line and there were similar structures on the approaches to several other tunnels, including Clayton and Wellhead. *(M. Teale)*

Unlike the railway formation seen on the previous page, from which track had recently been recovered, the section with track still in situ between Hainworth Lane and the Haincliffe Road at Ingrow has grown into a jungle after years of disuse. This view is looking towards Ingrow station, where the Bradford and Halifax the platform can just be seen under the bridge. The high retaining wall on the right continued for about 50 yards to the abutment of the Hainworth Lane stone arch bridge, from which this photograph was taken in May 1965. The full height of this impressive structure was lost in 2016 when the railway cutting to Ingrow Tunnel on the other side of Hainworth Lane was infilled. However, the retaining wall and the approach to the bridge itself was only half filled as that section was needed to gain access to the main works in the cutting. No further work had been done at the time of writing. *(John Rothera)*

Ingrow East station had been closed to passengers for ten years when this photograph was taken on 13 September 1965 – and it certainly shows. All stations on the lines from Bradford and Halifax were left to deteriorate after closure to passengers in May 1955 but, by this time, only Ingrow and Ovenden remained standing. Part of Ovenden station still survives in private use but the decrepit buildings at Ingrow were finally put out of their misery in 1966. Most photographers tended to record Ingrow East station looking towards Keighley from the Haincliffe Road bridge but this less common view has been taken from the station's wrought iron footbridge and is looking south. The staircase from Haincliffe Road to the Bradford and Halifax platform can be clearly seen but the staircase to the Keighley platform is out of view, although it was still in place at this time. In GNR and LNER days, the station was simply known as Ingrow but 'East' was added by British Railways in 1951 to distinguish it from the Worth Valley station which became Ingrow West. *(KWVR Archive)*

The one-mile section from Keighley to Ingrow East was retained for freight when the line to Cullingworth closed in 1956. The yard was then served by a Bradford Manningham locomotive out-based at Keighley. The sub shed closed in June 1962 when goods traffic on the Worth Valley branch was withdrawn and, after that, workings to and from Ingrow East became part of the Manningham J93 diagram which also served the yards at Bingley, Steeton and Kildwick. Revenue from Ingrow remained steady and between September 1963 and August 1964, it received 607 wagonloads of freight (457 coal and 150 cement/building materials) amounting to 5,456 tons which earned £6,610 in revenue (£96,000 in today's money). However, Ingrow was on the radar of BR management, along with Thornton and Great Horton which had also survived the earlier closures. This time, they weren't so lucky and all three yards closed on 28 June 1965. The annual savings in Ingrow's case were put at £2,395 (£29,000 today). This view, recorded two weeks before the final train, shows the line descending towards Woodhouse Road bridge. The building in the middle distance is the water tower associated with the GNR Ingrow locomotive shed which closed in 1936 and later became a store for an iron foundry, then a cash and carry warehouse. The tower was demolished in 1985 and the former loco shed followed in 1990. *(John Rothera)*

In the summer of 1957, Ivatt 2-6-2T No. 41326 and its three-coach 'motor train' from Oxenhope come to a stand at Keighley GN Junction signal box where driver at the far end prepares to hand over the Worth Valley branch single line token to the signalman. Each end of the 'motor train' had a driving compartment and apparatus was fitted to the locomotive to allow 'push-pull' working, thereby avoiding the need for uncoupling and running round at Oxenhope and Keighley. On the right is the GNR connection to the Midland Railway's Worth Valley line, which was double track into the shared Keighley passenger station. At the time of this view, the connection was only open for freight to the former GN yards at Ingrow East and Keighley as the line to Cullingworth had been closed to all traffic a year earlier. The tunnel which can be seen on the extreme right takes the former GNR goods lines under Park Lane and into the extensive Keighley South yard. *(Peter Sunderland)*

The Worth Valley branch 'motor train' climbs from Keighley, having just passed the junction with the GN line to Bradford and Halifax via Queensbury. Originally, this was a double track junction but the connection was singled in 1942. This locomotive was a regular on Worth Valley trains from 1957 until DMUs took over in June 1960. These versatile tank engines were designed by the Chief Mechanical Engineer of the London, Midland & Scottish Railway Company, Henry Ivatt, but only ten had been delivered by the time the LMS disappeared with railway Nationalisation in 1948. The rest of the 130-strong class were built by British Railways, including 41326 which was 'push-pull' fitted from new. It emerged from Derby Works in 1952 and was allocated to Skipton. When seen here in July 1957, it had recently been transferred to Bradford Manningham and is carrying its newly-fitted 55F shed plate. Having been ousted from its local duties, 41326 moved to Brighton in September 1961 and was withdrawn from there in May 1964 after a service life of only 12 years. *(Peter Sunderland)*

It is 31 July 1965 and this Great Northern Railway locomotive has returned briefly to former GNR metals. The scene is from the early days of the Keighley & Worth Valley Railway Preservation Society - three years before it ran its first public trains - and shows Gresley N2 class 0-6-2T No. 4744 (in LNER livery) preparing to propel coaches back down the line towards Keighley. GN Junction signal box had been downgraded to a shunting frame in June 1962 and the points were locked to leave just a single line through Platform 3 at Keighley station to Ingrow East, which was still open for freight. As a precaution, a rail had also been removed between GN Junction and the point where the Worth Valley line became single track. It was therefore necessary for this stock movement to proceed towards Ingrow East on the GN connecting line, then set back towards Platform 4 at Keighley before going forward towards Haworth. A ganger can just be seen behind the train, barring and clamping the points. Ingrow East goods yard had closed a month earlier. The locomotive was a product of the North British Locomotive Company and entered service in February 1921. It was withdrawn in September 1962 as BR No. 69523 and became the only one of its type to enter preservation. At the time of writing, it was based on the North Norfolk Railway. *(Peter Sunderland)*

Ivatt No. 41326 again, this time setting out from Keighley on a Worth Valley train for Oxenhope in September 1959. It is passing the perimeter of the former GNR goods yard – by this time known as Keighley South to distinguish it from the ex-Midland Railway depot across the road which had become Keighley North. Both depots had been renamed in 1951 as part of the same BR directive which saw the two Ingrow stations become East and West, as referred to on Page 102. Keighley West signal box can be seen above the end of the train. *(Peter Sunderland)*

Having secured the view seen on the previous page, photographer Peter Sunderland immediately turned his camera to record 41326 heading away towards Ingrow West. The sidings in the ex-GNR yard on the right are well filled with wagons but this does not necessarily reflect how busy it was for 'normal' everyday traffic as some of these vehicles were condemned and awaiting scrapping. In fact, the yard had been on a hiding to nothing since the 'through' freight over the Queensbury line was withdrawn in May 1956. Although freight from Halifax and Bradford continued to run to Keighley using the Laisterdyke-Idle-Windhill line, which joined the former Midland main line at Shipley Junction, access into the Keighley South yard required two reversals which was time consuming and inefficient. Trains destined for the yard had to be tripped across from Keighley North, then up the Worth Valley branch to GN Junction where they were reversed again down the goods line to reach their destination. As freight revenue at Keighley South dwindled, BR management approved the removal of surplus sidings in September 1960. They then decided to concentrate all Keighley freight business at the former Midland depot and the old GNR yard closed in July 1961. *(Peter Sunderland)*

Competition for freight business between the Midland and Great Northern Railway companies at Keighley was fierce. The Midland had been established in the town since the 1840s and had enjoyed a monopoly in both freight and passenger revenues. The arrival of the GNR forty years later changed all that and the company did not scrimp on the provision of facilities in its new goods yard which was bigger than that of its rival. Twelve sidings were laid, three of which went into this large two-storey warehouse which had entrances from East Parade and here in Low Mill Lane. It survives today as premises for a builders' merchants' business. This view, taken on 25 July 1967, still shows the building's former London & North Eastern Railway Company identity dating from the 1920s when the GNR was absorbed following the Railway Grouping Act of 1921. No trace of this inscription remains today. In addition to the main warehouse, two single-storey goods sheds were built just off East Parade as a later expansion of the yard. These survived in private use for more than 50 years after closure but were demolished in the winter of 2012-13. The yard also had a stable block for 24 delivery cart horses which was still standing in 2020.

(HMRS John Bateman Collection)

Ivatt No. 41273 awaits departure from Platform 3 at Keighley station with a Worth Valley service to Ingrow West, Oakworth, Haworth and Oxenhope in 1958. This platform - and Platform 4, from which this photograph was taken - were shared by Worth Valley trains and those bound for Halifax and Bradford via Queensbury from November 1884 until May 1955 when the latter were withdrawn. (John Carter)

PLATFORM Nº4

CROSS THE LINE BY THE SUBWAY
FOR SKIPTON BRADFORD & LEEDS TRAINS

Another view from Platform 4 at Keighley station two years later and 41273 is still one of the regular Worth Valley engines – but not for much longer. It is seen here with an afternoon service for Oxenhope on 30 May 1960, a few weeks before the branch services were taken over by DMUs. The old wooden signage, over-painted in BR's familiar North Eastern Region colours, advises passengers from Worth Valley services to cross the line by the subway for Skipton, Bradford and Leeds trains. Anyone who might have fancied the scenic route to Bradford via Queensbury would have been five years too late. (J.C.W. Halliday)

After demolition of the 'Queensbury Lines,' land was sold off, cuttings were infilled and new developments obliterated many parts of the old track bed, especially in urban areas. However, several miles of the more rural sections survived, although heavily overgrown. Keen to protect what was left, this book's authors, Alan Whitaker and Jan Rapacz, developed a proposal for a 'Great Northern Railway Trail' and, at the invitation of the then Lord Mayor of Bradford, Councillor Stanley King, presented their ideas to senior officials and elected representatives at City Hall in July 2000. The principal aim was to safeguard the magnificent viaducts at Thornton and Hewenden by creating a footpath and cycleway using the former railway. A similar idea had been aired by the Keighley MP, Bob Cryer, 20 years earlier but had come to nothing. Among those who attended the City Hall presentation was senior planning officer, Jeff McQuillan, who became pivotal in securing Council support for the scheme. Following his retirement, he became Chair of a liaison group to promote the Trail and has led it ever since. This book's authors have been members of the group from the start and three miles of the GNRT are now open to the public. The first - from Cullingworth to the Wilsden station site - was opened by SUSTRANS on 23 May 2005, exactly 50 years after closure to passenger services. Other sections opened in stages between 2007 and 2013 to complete the link from Thornton to Queensbury. This photograph shows the opening of the Thornton Viaduct section on 20 November 2008, with the support of children from Thornton Primary School which occupies the former goods yard and station site. Efforts to close the gap between Thornton and Wilsden are continuing. *(Jan Rapacz)*